BLITZKRIEG RUSSIA

IMAGES OF WAR
BLITZKRIEG RUSSIA

RARE PHOTOGRAPHS FROM WARTIME ARCHIVES

Jonathan Sutherland and Diane Canwell

Pen & Sword
MILITARY

First published in Great Britain in 2011 by
PEN & SWORD MILITARY
An imprint of
Pen & Sword Books Ltd
47 Church Street
Barnsley
South Yorkshire
S70 2AS

ISBN 978-1-84884-334-9

Typeset by Concept, Huddersfield, West Yorkshire
Printed and bound in England by CPI UK

Pen & Sword Books Ltd incorporates the imprints of Pen & Sword Aviation, Pen & Sword Maritime, Pen & Sword Military, Wharncliffe Local History, Pen & Sword Select, Pen & Sword Military Classics, Leo Cooper, Remember When, Seaforth Publishing and Frontline Publishing.

For a complete list of Pen & Sword titles please contact
PEN & SWORD BOOKS LIMITED
47 Church Street, Barnsley, South Yorkshire, S70 2AS, England
E-mail: enquiries@pen-and-sword.co.uk
Website: www.pen-and-sword.co.uk

Contents

Introduction

Operation *Barbarossa* shattered the early hours of 22 June 1941 as four immense German panzer groups, supported by hundreds of thousands of infantry, massed artillery and a curtain of air cover, struck at the Soviet Union. The Russians knew it was coming, there had been tell-tale signs for weeks, but inexplicably, Stalin had prevented his forces from taking any countermeasures. The German attacks were split between three vast Army Groups:

- Army Group North under Field Marshal Ritter von Leeb, consisting of twenty-six divisions, including three panzer divisions.
- Army Group Centre under Field Marshal Fedor von Bock consisted of fifty-one divisions, including nine panzer divisions.
- Army Group South under Field Marshal Gerd von Rundstedt consisted of fifty-nine divisions, including five panzer divisions, fourteen Rumanian and three Hungarian.

These Army Groups were supported by three air fleets boasting over 3,000 aircraft, and a fourth air fleet operating in the far north:

- *Luftflotte* I under Colonel General Alfred Keller, supporting Army Group North.
- *Luftflotte* II under Field Marshal Albert Kesselring, supporting Army Group Centre.
- *Luftflotte* IV under Colonel General Alexander Löhr, supporting Army Group South.
- *Luftflotte* V under Colonel General Hans-Jürgen Stumpff, supporting the mountain troops aiming to strike at Murmansk.

The Soviet Union had a population of some 190 million, of which 16 million were of military age. If the frontier defences could be held and the German penetrations kept to a minimum, it would only be a matter of time before the Russians could mobilize their vast resources. We have a somewhat false image of the German Army crossing into Russian-held Poland and other points along the frontier. The cutting edge was tanks and armoured fighting vehicles, along with expensively trained and equipped *panzergrenadiers*, but the bulk of the force would have had to advance at a much more sedate pace. Mobility-wise, they were no more advanced than the French troops that had invaded Russian nearly 130 years before. The bulk of the men would have to march on foot and the reliance on the horse (some 750,000) was still immense. Of the 153 divisions that were involved in the invasion, 119 still had horse-drawn transport.

Facing them were three large groups or Military Districts with massive potential reserves:

- On the Baltic front, the Russian forces consisted of twenty-four divisions, of which four were armoured.
- Opposite the Pripet Marshes were thirty divisions with eight armoured.
- Around Kiev there were fifty-eight divisions, sixteen of which were armoured.
- On the Rumanian border were twelve divisions, four of which were armoured.

Not only were these units not deployed to fight a defensive campaign, but some were as much as 300 miles to the rear and would take days to reach the front. As it was, by 23 June the Germans had penetrated some 62 miles into Russian-held Poland; they had bypassed the vast fortress at Brest-Litovsk on the River Bug (it would surrender on 24 July).

On 3 July, Stalin broadcast to his people:

Comrades, citizens, brothers and sisters, men of the Army and Navy! I speak to you my friends. A grave threat hangs over our country. It can only be dispersed by the combined efforts of the military and industrial might of the nation. There is no room for the timid or the coward, for deserters or spreaders of panic, and a merciless struggle must be waged against such people. History shows us that there are no invincible armies. The enemy must not find a single railway-wagon, not a wagon, not a pound of bread or a glassful of petrol. All the *Kolkhozes* [collective farms] must bring in their herds and hand their stocks of wheat over to official bodies to be sent to the rear. Everything that is usable but cannot be sent back must be destroyed.

On the very day that the broadcast was made the pocket of resistance at Bialystock was reduced and surrendered. Some 290,000 Russians were taken prisoner, 2,500 tanks destroyed and 1,500 artillery pieces taken. Just six days later, the Germans had overwhelmed Latvia, Lithuania, and the bulk of Estonia, and taken Minsk, trapping another 300,000 Russian troops. The outskirts of Kiev were reached on 11 July. The Germans encircled it, and thanks to Stalin's decree that the city should be held at all costs, another 665,000 prisoners, 900 tanks and 3,179 artillery pieces were taken.

On 22 July, 127 German aircraft hit the Soviet capital, Moscow. Five days later, the Germans pushed towards Leningrad, which would have to withstand a siege of 900 days before Russian troops beat their way through to the fortress city; by that time some 800,000 city dwellers would have perished.

The relentless progress of the German advance showed no signs of slowing up; by 5 August, the pocket around Smolensk had surrendered, bagging 510,000 prisoners. Two days later, the Uman pocket surrendered and another 100,000 men surrendered. Although this all made grim reading, the Germans were beginning to realize the true costs of taking on the Russians. In the period September 1939 to May 1941, taking all of the campaigns into account, the Germans had suffered 218,109 casualties, of which 97,000 were killed. As 15 August dawned, the sobering news was that in the first fifty-three days of the war with Russia there had been 389,924 casualties, of which 98,600 were dead.

At the beginning of September 1941, Hitler decreed that the primary target must be Moscow. Armoured units that had been transferred to the north and the south were to be returned and Army Group Centre was to go hell-for-leather for the Soviet capital. Although the capital would never fall, had it done so, it would have been a massive blow to the Russians, perhaps knocking them out of the war before the United States joined. The capture of the city would have effectively split the country in two, making communications between the north and south impossible.

As we know, a combination of over-ambitiousness on the part of the Germans, simply unable to comprehend the vast distances and spaces and their effect on supply and reinforcement, the weather and, of course, the stubborn resistance of the Russians, all conspired to preserve Russia. *Barbarossa* was arguably the last and the greatest *blitzkrieg* campaign, flawed by its sheer size and over-elaboration. *Blitzkrieg Russia* chronicles the early stages of Germany's war with Russia: the successes, the overwhelming power of the advance, and the crippling losses suffered by the Russians.

We have selected the best photographs from five albums, which focus on that first year of war in the East, now in the collection of James Payne. Unfortunately, only one of the albums is named, that of Josef Kaloenbach, who may well have been a German driver, as he can be seen in a number of different vehicles. The identity of the other owners will remain a mystery, but the sights that they have captured on their cameras reveal the true extent and horror of this phase of the Second World War. It was at a time when the Germans seemed to be invincible, having overrun the countries of Western Europe, with only Britain standing alone to defy her. In switching his attention to the east to once and for all eradicate Russia and communism, Hitler had embarked on the greatest mistake of the war. It would end in ignominious defeat in barely four years from the time when the first German aircraft, vehicles and troops crossed into Russian-held Poland.

Chapter 1

Josef Kaloenbach's Album

The Germans began planning for Operation *Barbarossa* literally within weeks of the French surrender. By the end of July 1940, planning was nearing completion and the *Aufbau Ost* (build-up east) had already begun.

The first photograph in this small collection seems to imply that in July 1940 Josef Kaloenbach was at Greifswald in north-eastern Germany, some 150 miles from Berlin. Greifswald was a major railway hub and housed an enormous army garrison. We can therefore make the reasonable assumption that the photographs that belong to this album may well refer to his duties with Army Group North during the operations against Russia.

Army Group North's target was Leningrad, some 500 miles away. Hoepner's Panzer Group would provide the cutting edge to slice through the Russian frontier defences and make for the River Dvina and then onward to Opochka. (Hoepner was a career officer and an early supporter of armoured warfare. He was later implicated in the July 1944 plot to assassinate Hitler and was executed in the August.) From then on, depending on the state of Leningrad's defences, they would advance north or north-east. The 18th Army would be tasked with clearing the Baltic region and the 16th Army would secure the connection with Army Group Centre.

The Russians wrongly believed that Leningrad would only be under threat from the Finns and the Germans from the north and that the main German attacks would be launched against Moscow. However, in mid-November 1940 they discovered through intelligence sources that the Germans were planning to launch an assault from the west, toward Leningrad. Unfortunately, neither the Russian Baltic Special Military District nor, indeed, the Leningrad Military District did very much to re-organize for this anticipated attack.

The Germans had eleven months to prepare for the invasion. The Russians believed that they would have at least ten to fifteen days' prior notice before any assault was launched.

Army Group North had some twenty-nine divisions, plus a further five German divisions and fifteen Finnish divisions. A great deal has been written about *blitzkrieg* tactics, but, in fact, it was the logical successor to the traditional Prussian war of manoeuvre. *Blitzkrieg* itself can be described as the use of mechanized units, a flexible command structure, the control of units using radio communication and the close support and cooperation of air assets.

In the north, 4th Panzer Group had two panzer corps. Each of the panzer divisions had between two and three panzer battalions, supported by five infantry battalions and three artillery battalions. The motorized infantry were used in close cooperation with the panzer units. The type of tanks being used by the Germans at this stage was a mix of Panzer IIIs and Panzer IVs. However, many of the units still had Panzer IIs, which were being used as a stopgap measure as the Panzer IIIs and IVs were delivered. There were also considerable numbers of 38Ts, which were Czech-built tanks, broadly equivalent to the Panzer III. In fact, the 8th Panzer Division had 118 of these vehicles. The 6th Panzer Division was also saddled with fairly obsolete 35Ts, with 155 of these vehicles in use.

While many of the mechanized units had either self-propelled artillery or vehicle-towed pieces, most of the infantry divisions' artillery was horse-drawn. This was inevitably going to be a major problem, particularly for the infantry units trying to keep pace with the faster-moving mechanised units.

Even at this stage of the war, supply was also a major problem. Supposedly, Army Group North was due to receive thirty-four train loads of supplies per day, but the best that was ever achieved was eighteen. Compounding the problem was the vast array of different vehicles. One of the artillery regiments in Army Group North had nearly seventy different types of vehicle, which meant that providing spare parts and carrying out maintenance was incredibly difficult.

The *Luftwaffe*, in direct support, was using Bf 109 fighters, Ju87 Stuka dive-bombers, Heinkel 111 bombers and Ju52 transport planes. Of the three *Luftflotten* supporting Operation *Barbarossa*, *Luftflotte* I was the smallest. They were supposed to have some support from *Luftflotte* V, based in Norway, but in practical terms, due to the enormous operational area, very little help was actually given. This meant that the Russian Air Force actually outnumbered the *Luftwaffe* in Army Group North's area of operations. They had a seven to one superiority in fighters and a three to one superiority in bombers.

Ground defence units in Army Group North were weak, with only three flak regiments. The only other contribution from the *Luftwaffe* was the use of the 7th *Flieger* Division, which had been dropped on Crete and had suffered appalling casualties in May 1941. They were used around Shlisselburg between September and December 1941. The other supporting element was the *Kriegsmarine*, the German navy. Their Baltic force was not very impressive: four light cruisers, five U-boats, around forty patrol boats and a number of other minelayers and sweepers. There were also a handful of Finnish vessels. The Germans began mining the gulfs of Finland and Riga in mid-June 1941. Their only other responsibility was to prevent Russian vessels from getting out of the Baltic, or being involved in amphibious operations.

The Russians called Army Group North's area of front the North-West Front. The Russians had twenty-four divisions and five brigades, amounting to nearly 370,000 men. In addition, there were a further nineteen divisions arrayed against the Finns and the Germans.

As we will see in this album and in future photographs, the Russians had an enormous number of tanks. However, the vast majority of them were obsolete by 1941. Having said that, many of them were still equal to what the Germans would field. Initially, the Russians would deploy the majority of their tanks in an infantry support role, rather than concentrating them into mechanized corps. In fact, there had been a great deal of confusion; after Poland had fallen in 1939 the Russians had disbanded their mechanized corps. Once France had fallen in May 1940, they recreated them again. In the six months leading up to the launching of Operation *Barbarossa*, the Russians were feverishly trying to create twenty new mechanized corps.

The scene was now set for a titanic struggle. During the period in which these photographs were taken there was an almost unbroken run of German victories and humiliating Russian defeats.

This is a fascinating photograph of a German artillery crew towing, using only their muscles, an 88mm Flak gun toward the parade ground at Greifswald. The photograph is dated July 1940. There is a tantalising glimpse of another artillery piece in the right foreground. The Germans would produce many thousands of these 88mm Flak guns and in due course they would prove to be extremely efficient tank killers. The Flak gun had a characteristic cruciform gun carriage, which allowed the weapon to be fired in all directions. The weapon had been used during the Spanish Civil War, where it had already been noted that it was a useful anti-tank weapon and general artillery piece. It would see extensive service on the Eastern Front and was far more effective than other weapons, particularly in the early stage of the war, when the majority of German tanks could only boast a 37mm or a 50mm gun.

This particular weapon appears to be a Flak 36; it entered service between 1936 and 1937 and had a redesigned trailer, known as the Sonderanhänger 202. It was a new design and had twin wheels on two similarly shaped carriages. It could actually engage ground targets from the trailer mounted position. Its weight was around 7 tons and the weapon had a rate of fire of up to twenty rounds per minute. This particular version does not have the characteristic shield to protect the crew, although the majority of these weapons would later be fitted with them.

Russian bodies and debris alongside a road are shown here. The German column of supply and infantry trucks has halted. The speed of the advance was crippling; there were long days and short nights and a lot of marching and fighting. As a prime example, the 291st Infantry Division advanced 40 miles on 22 June 1941. Infantry and mechanized units would ride to battle, but fight on foot. For the majority of the German infantry, everything was on foot. The manpower and resources assigned to the German Army more often than not came a poor fourth after the SS, the *Luftwaffe* and the panzer troops. In many respects, the German infantry that crossed the frontier into war in the east in 1941 were little different from those that had invaded Poland in 1939. Usually, infantry battalions attached to the panzer divisions would be truck mounted and one battalion would be on motorcycles.

This is a grim but fascinating photograph, which shows a knocked out or abandoned Russian T34 with two dead crewmembers. A large German motorized column is passing along the tree-lined road. The T34/76A had gone into full production in June 1940. It would be the major Russian tank of the Second World War, with many different production models and variants. It was the most advanced design of its time and had the Russians concentrated their armour then the losses that the Germans would suffer would have been even greater. Although it had fully sloped armour, it was very easy to build. In fact, it was fairly unsophisticated and easy to maintain and it also had a low silhouette. Although we cannot see the front of the tank, the early versions had a second machine gun in a turret ball mount. The main armament was a 76.2mm gun. The T34 was virtually impervious to normal 37mm and 50mm anti-tank gun shells. It outclassed the Panzer III and was even as good as the Panzer IV, although later versions of the Panzer IV were arguably slightly better. It would prove to be a serious headache for the Germans.

A panoramic shot of German panzers, advancing across a Russian plain, can be seen in this photograph. If we are correct in our assumption that these photographs were taken in the northern sector of the attack, then these are likely to have belonged to the 8th Panzer Division. By the evening of 23 June 1941, the 1st Panzer Division had captured a vital railway bridge at Tytuvenai, and the 6th Panzer Division had outrun its logistical support and was running short of ammunition. In fact, it had failed to force a crossing of the River Dubysa, and instead had to take up defensive positions near Raseiniai in order to fend off over a hundred Russian tanks. The motorcycle infantry battalion was wiped out in twenty minutes. Responding to the danger, the 1st Panzer Division was ordered to halt and head east to support the 6th. This was the spearhead of the Panzer Corps and the Germans battled with KVIs at ranges fewer than thirty yards. The tank battle reached its crucial stage on 25 June; the 1st Panzer Division's command post was almost overwhelmed, but it was still battling through to save the 6th Panzer Division. Much of the Russian 3rd Mechanised Corps was trapped and the 12th Mechanized Corps was destroyed soon afterwards. In fact, the 12th, which had mustered 690 tanks on 22 June, had barely fifty left by the end of the month.

This is a second panoramic shot of German tanks advancing across the Russian plains. Meanwhile, more German tanks, supported by *Panzergrenadiers*, were streaking across Latvia. By the evening of 27 June, the Russians were attempting to launch counterattacks. There was a dangerous 75-mile gap, which isolated LVI Panzer Corps. The Russian air force flew over 2,000 sorties against the units and the Germans responded by destroying at least 200 Russian tanks.

This is a truly impressive line-up of SdKfzs sporting flak artillery pieces. The SdKfz was a hard-track military vehicle, which dates back to 1934 when designs were underway, leading to its first appearance in 1938. Aside from being a tractor for the 88mm Flak gun and howitzers, it was also widely used as a self-propelled anti-aircraft vehicle, with either 20mm or 37mm Flak guns. While the vehicle was produced in enormous numbers, there were never enough of them. Artillery elements of panzer divisions and *Panzergrenadier* units tended to get the first supplies, while most of the other units had to rely on horses.

In all, some 12,187 of these vehicles were produced by March 1945. Production in the early years of the war had been at its peak in 1939 when over 1,600 were built. The production rate dropped in 1940 to just fewer than 1,000, but rose again to 1,300 in 1941. The majority of the vehicles were produced in Berlin, Bremen, Munich and later in Vienna and in Italian factories.

German truck drivers pose in front of one of their vehicles in this photograph. Clearly, one of these men must be Josef Kaloenbach. The most common German military truck produced for the war was a 3-ton Opel Blitz. Essentially, it was a cargo truck and over 100,000 of them were built. It had a characteristic lightning emblem on the front radiator panel. Huge numbers of these trucks were needed and many other variants of the vehicle were made, from fire trucks to buses. There were also Mercedes-built trucks, which were almost identical. The truck was extremely popular; it was integral to panzer divisions; notably it used gasoline, the same fuel used by the tanks, which made it an ideal partner. The gasoline engine could be easily defrosted with boiled water in very cold conditions, whereas trucks fuelled by diesel were much more difficult to start. The truck was undoubtedly the backbone of the *Wehrmacht*.

German infantrymen, with field caps, ammunition pouches and, on the floor in front of them, their backpacks, bedroll and characteristic German helmet, can be seen here. The men are wearing M1938 field service caps in field grey cloth. They were designed so that both sides could be pulled down and worn around the ears. The sides of the cap, towards the front, are scalloped to allow clearer vision when the cap is worn with the sides down. It was also designed to be worn under the steel helmet.

The men also appear to be wearing black leather marching boots and M1936 single-breasted service tunics, made from a mixture of wool and rayon. The collars are faced in a dark blue/green material, which was also used as a backing cloth for the national emblem, worn on the right breast of the jacket.

The backpack was known as a *tornister* and was worn by normal infantry. A rucksack was used by motorised infantry. The *tornister* was in general use until the end of the war. It is likely that these were M95 patterns, with four small leather straps, although the M34 version did not have straps to hold a mess kit.

Young German soldiers relax in a straw field barn here. Note the collection of equipment hanging from the walls, including gas masks, backpacks, bread sacks, various belts and steel helmets. The men appear to be wearing denim fatigue jackets and trousers, which appear to be of a darker material than their standard uniforms. In all probability these men wore these to drive the vehicles and to carry out maintenance and repairs. There is notably an absence of any sign of weapons. Panzer units wore red/green denims, with large patch pockets. It was designed to be hardwearing, lightweight and easy to wash.

Another posed shot here; this time we can clearly see the hobnail soles of the German soldiers' footwear. The men are wearing black leather marching boots, or *Marschstiefel*. Whilst this type of footwear would have been ideal for the spring or summer periods on the eastern front, as the weather started to deteriorate towards the end of 1941 there was a dire need for heavy-duty, winter footwear. Initially, compressed and moulded felt was introduced as an over boot. These were a combination of thick felt and leather but they could also be made from thick layers of plaited straw, which were designed to be large enough to fit over the normal marching boot.

One of the drivers poses beside a Horch Kfz15 staff car in this photograph. The vehicle was used primarily as a communications vehicle. They were built by Mercedes-Benz, with six-cylinder petrol engines. It was also used as a light troop transport and command car and was more spacious and versatile than the Kubelwagen. This particular vehicle appears to be painted in the standard German grey and at this stage of the war lacks camouflage. An interim camouflage of sand yellow was introduced later in the war, to break up the profile of the vehicle.

This photograph shows what appears to be a T34/76, which has presumably come to grief after crushing a car beneath it. There were innumerable versions of the T34. This version of the tank ceased with the T34/76F, with just 100 vehicles of this version produced as the up-gunned T34/85 came into production in 1944. In all, nearly 85,000 T34s were produced and while it was designed and improved in the late 1930s and early 1940s, it would actually remain in production until 1958.

This is a motorcycle despatch rider, resting on his machine in front of a Horch Kfz15. German motorcycles were built to be robust and reliable. The two stripes on this man's arm signify that he is a *gefreiter*. The man also appears to be wearing an Infantry Assault Badge in bronze, for motorized infantry. This would be worn on the left breast pocket and was instituted on 20 December 1939. The initial class was in silver and given to foot infantry that had participated in combat action. This meant that they had a degree of experience and qualified them for the badge. The bronze version was instituted on 1 June 1940 and there were similar criteria. There was, however, one notable distinction; a bronzed version was given to motorized panzer troops and silver to standard infantry units.

A knocked-out or abandoned T34 is shown here. The T34/76B had a welded turret and a long M1940 76.2mm gun. It had broad tracks that gave it low ground pressure and had a powerful 500hp diesel engine, giving it a maximum speed on the road of 53km/h. It had a range of around 400km.

Another knocked-out T34, with two members of Kaloenbach's unit posing in front of it. In the Russian Baltic (Special) Military District, which ran along the border with East Prussia, operating with the 8th Army, was the XII Mechanized Corps. There was also the III Mechanized Corps with the 11th Army. The XII could muster some 651 tanks out of their establishment strength of 1,031. The III could put around 500 into battle. Around 105 of the 1,150 or so tanks available were newer models; nearly all were KV1s and KV2s.

A downed Russian aircraft, which appears to be a Tupolev SB. Some 94 per cent of the Russian army air force bombers were SBs by June 1941. It was a twin-engine, three-seat monoplane that was advanced in design but lacking in a great deal of refinement. It has been estimated that some 6,656 of these aircraft were built, having been introduced in 1936. The aircraft remained in production until 1941. It could carry around 600kg of bombs and as a defensive armament it had six 7.62mm machine guns and had a crew of three.

This sobering photograph shows the true extent of the Russians' failure to prepare themselves for the German onslaught that was Operation *Barbarossa*. These Russian prisoners of war, at this early stage, are relatively fortunate, as it is clear that they have been fed. The Germans did not apply the same standard of treatment to Russian prisoners as they had to the British, French and others that they had captured in the west. Between 1941 and 1945, around 5.7 million Russian prisoners were captured by the Germans. Around one million of these were released during the war; half a million either escaped or were liberated by their own countrymen. Some 930,000 were alive in camps at the end of the war. The remaining 3.3 million died during captivity. Figures are often disputed, but even by conservative standards upwards of 2.5 million Russians died in labour camps.

This is the classic German R12 motorcycle with sidecar. Between 1935 and 1942, some 36,000 were built. The majority of the ones destined for military service were equipped with the sidecar. They were often used by units designed to penetrate gaps in the enemy front and make penetrating raids behind the lines; effectively they would motorize a light reconnaissance unit. The Russians were so impressed with German motorcycle combinations that they copied it; in fact, there was a Russian version of the BMW R71, known as the M72. The Russian version was in some respects superior and it is still being manufactured in China today.

Set against a panoramic background, this is the SdKfz7 with a Flak gun mounted. It has what appears to be a 37mm Flak gun, which used a mechanical bolt for automatic fire and could fire off around 160 rounds per minute. The 37mm Flak 18 entered service in 1935 and ceased production in 1936, to be replaced by the Flak 36, which was easier to use in action. There was another variant, the Flak 37, but the only difference was that this version was fitted with a better sight, which was powered by clockwork. Both the Flak 36 and 37 were produced in enormous numbers. After 1940 they had become the standard defence weapon against low-flying enemy aircraft. They were usually organized into nine or twelve gun batteries.

Three of the truck drivers are on fatigue duty here. The men are wearing practical and easy-to-keep-clean, hard-wearing fatigue uniforms. It appears from this photograph that the men are collecting hay, which suggests that a significant proportion of the unit were not motorized, but in fact still horse drawn.

A close-up of the cab of an SdKfz7, with its flak gun's mantle showing that it has netting around it, which could be used to fix camouflage. Also note that the canopy over the cab is canvas, as is the door to the driver's side. Canvas has also been pulled across the windscreen. In the right foreground of the photograph are stowed and protected Gewehr 98, 7.92mm standard issue rifles. The Germans believed that this rifle was really too long and bulky for front-line use, which led to the introduction of the Karabiner 98B. The major changes were to the bolt handle, the sling swivels and the ability to use better ammunition.

This photograph was presumably taken somewhat later in 1941, possibly in October, after the first torrential rains had begun. Two of the men are wearing German Army greatcoats; there were at least thirteen different styles worn during the war. These appear to be standard pattern field grey, with dark blue/green collars. It was actually designed and introduced before the war began. It was a long, double-breasted garment that had two rows of six field grey metal buttons. It was slightly waisted, which gave a flare to the bottom of the coat. There were two slash pockets set at a slight angle with rounded pocket flaps. They had 15cm deep turn back cuffs. The greatcoat was correctly worn buttoned up to the neck, as can be seen on the man on the extreme left of the photograph. The collar was fastened with the neck hood and folded down in place. The collar could be turned up around the wearer's neck and lower jaw and secured by a small cloth flap.

This is a truly fascinating photograph that shows a German balloon. This appears to be a German observation balloon, which had been used extensively during the First World War. The observer was suspended in a basket, with a wireless set, binoculars and a long-range camera. His role was to observe the front and behind it and to spot enemy troop movements and concentrations, so that he could call down artillery fire. These balloons would have been well protected with anti-aircraft guns.

Chapter 2

The *Panzergrenadiers*

The photographs in this chapter are a fascinating and evocative selection, which appear to have belonged to a member of the *Panzergrenadier* unit operating in Russia in 1941. Predominantly, there are photographs of knocked out or abandoned Russian tanks and there is certainly significant indication that these *Panzergrenadiers* were at the forefront of the battles in 1941. It is unfortunate that we know neither the unit nor the location of any of these photographs.

The term *Panzergrenadier* literally means motorized, or mechanized, infantry. In fact, the term was not really adopted until 1942. The infantry that were attached to panzer divisions prior to this were known as *Schützen* regiments. The *Panzergrenadiers* were trained to fight combined arms warfare. They would usually be truck mounted and operating with a battalion of tanks, along with artillery, reconnaissance units, anti-tank and anti-aircraft artillery and combat engineers.

Contrary to popular opinion, the *Panzergrenadiers* did not tend to be mounted in SdKfz251 troop carriers, as they were in relatively short supply and only went to elite divisions first. The vast majority of the men were truck mounted.

By the beginning of 1942 the typical *Panzergrenadier* battalion consisted of a headquarters unit, a heavy company, a machine gun company and three motorized rifle companies. The heavy company would have an anti-tank platoon of three towed 37mm guns and an infantry gun platoon with a pair of 75mm guns. There would also be three squads making up a pioneer platoon. The machine gun company had two platoons, each armed with four MG34s. They would also have a platoon of six 80mm mortars. The rifle companies each had a section with two MG34s and three rifle platoons. The platoon had a headquarters unit, a 50mm mortar team and three squads, each with a pair of light machine guns. There were significant changes towards the end of 1941, but this is beyond the scope of the photographs in the collection.

Although there was a regulation way of wearing personal equipment, as we will see in this collection of photographs there is considerable variation. In many of the cases the men appear to be wearing their full kit, with the exception of their large packs. This would include a small pack, respirator case and entrenching tool, all of which were attached to their belts.

(Above) This is an abandoned Russian KB2. It appears that this monstrous tank was under tow before being abandoned. It was heavily armoured by contemporary standards, but it was incredibly slow and unstable. It sported a 152mm howitzer and an extra loader was required, in order to handle the heavy ammunition. There was 75mm of armour on the hull and 110mm on the turret. The total weight of the vehicle was 52 tons, the maximum road speed was around 26km/h and it had a maximum range of 250km. Due to its poor manoeuvrability and vulnerability, the vehicle was phased out at a fairly early stage of the war between Germany and Russia.

(Facing) The lead vehicle of a column of *Sturmgeschütz* (also known as StuGs), clattering along a road; they were designed for the close support of infantry in infantry, panzer and *Panzergrenadier* units. It is not a true tank, more of an assault gun. But in the early stages of Operation *Barbarossa*, particularly when facing Russian T34s, KV1s and KV2s, it was used in the anti-tank role. The first production vehicles, based on the Panzer III chassis, went into production in 1940. The vehicles had sloped superstructures made up of armour plates on a welded hull. They had greater frontal armour protection and sported short-barrelled 75mm guns. In August 1940, the *Sturmartillerie* units, as they were called, were organized into battalions, with eighteen assault guns in three, six-gun batteries. By March to April 1941, all of the batteries now had seven vehicles and by 1942 the longer-barrel 75mm guns were being introduced.

The StuG would undergo enormous changes and modifications to its superstructure, suspension, other equipment and weaponry over the years. It was operated by four crewmen; a commander, a gunner, a loader and radio operator and a driver.

One of the most famous StuG aces was Kurt Kirchnerof StuG Battalion 667. He destroyed thirty Russian tanks over the course of a few days in February 1942, in northern Russia, winning himself the Knight's Cross. Another ace of the period was Rudolf Jaenicke, who commanded a StuG platoon that destroyed twelve Russian BT2 tanks and numerous other vehicles that were loaded on rail platforms. This took place in the middle of July 1941. StuGs are credited with having destroyed as many as 20,000 enemy tanks by the beginning of 1944. There were over 1,200 still in service by the middle of April 1945, out of the 9,500 that had been produced to date.

This is a StuG, advancing through cover and followed by a section of *Panzergrenadiers*. The men are wearing their greatcoats. The original designation was for a 75mm assault gun on the StuG. A production order was placed, with deliveries to begin in September 1940, at a rate of fifty a month. They were built on the chassis of the Panzer III and designated SdKfz142. By the end of the winter of 1940 to 1941, 184 of these vehicles had been completed. Then came an improved engine and a third type, of which 548 were built, all of them with the short L/24 gun, as can be seen in this photograph. Shortly afterwards, there was an interim production model with the longer L/33 75mm gun, which was built largely due to experiences on the Russian front.

This photograph shows a pair of knocked out or abandoned Russian T26 tanks. The original T26 was a licence-built version of the Vickers 6-ton light tank. Later models were wholly Russian, with original design. These tanks are almost certainly T26B versions, which were developed for use with mechanized cavalry units. These had larger central turrets but were in essence very similar to the T26A. The tank had a 45mm gun and some models had as many as three 7.62mm machine guns. The vehicle had a maximum speed of 28km/h and a range of 375km, all on the road.

The final production version was the T26S, with thicker armour. The T26 was vulnerable to German anti-tank weapons, unlike some of its heavier counterparts. In fact, there were enormous numbers of these vehicles in the Russian ranks. The XIV Mechanized Corps, based around Brest Litovsk in the Western (Special) Military District, had an establishment of 1,025 tanks, which included 420 T34s and 126 KV tanks. Indeed, all that could really be mustered were 508 obsolete T26 tanks, which had been scavenged from various other units. This was a common situation for many of the Russian mechanized units.

A stricken and abandoned T34/76 is seen in this photograph. Although the Russians would lose a tremendous number of tanks, the Germans had seriously underestimated both Russian tank design and production capabilities. The Germans were quickly disabused of the situation when they encountered T34s and KV1 tanks. German tank design was rendered virtually obsolete.

The key advantage for the Russians was the simplicity of their tank design, which meant that they were easy to turn out in enormous numbers. Due to their overall simplicity, it was also possible for relatively inexperienced crews to operate them.

In the early stages of the war, their vulnerability was shown by the Russian tactic of using them as support weapons for infantry. This conspired to make it easier for the Germans to win engagements, offsetting the superiority of the Russian armour. As time passed, however, the Russians would adopt German mass tank formations and the Germans, in turn, would borrow a great deal from Russian tank design.

A group of *Panzergrenadiers* investigate a knocked out or abandoned T34 here. The German on the left of the photograph appears to be an officer, as he is carrying a map case around his neck. While Army Group North made for Leningrad via the Baltic states, Army Group Centre's pair of panzer groups thrust to the north and south of Brest Litovsk to converge to the east of Minsk. They reached the Beresina River in six days and then crossed the Dnieper River on 11 July. The next target was Smolensk, which fell to the Germans on 16 July. Fierce resistance around the city meant that a thrust toward Moscow had to be halted.

The German Army wanted to continue their offensive towards Moscow, but they were overruled; Hitler wanted the Ukraine in German hands, as it would net them a great deal of Russia's heavy industry, mining and agricultural resources. It is widely believed that this hold up in the assault against Moscow, often referred to as the 'summer pause', would ultimately lead to the Germans' failure to capture Moscow before the winter set it.

Another abandoned T34; two of the *Panzergrenadiers* have halted to take photographs, whilst the others trudge along off road in the distance. While Army Group Centre wrestled with Smolensk, it was Army Group South's responsibility to advance through Galicia and then into the Ukraine. Progress was comparatively slow, but by mid-July they had secured a route through to Kiev. Two Rumanian armies were advancing towards Odessa. Lead elements of the 1st Panzer Group advanced to join up with the southern flank of Army Group South at Uman; in the process 100,000 Russian soldiers were encircled. Huge numbers of Russian troops were also contained in a pocket to the east of Kiev and 400,000 of them fell into German hands when the city surrendered on 19 September 1941.

The Russians were desperately trying to evacuate as much heavy industry as they could, breaking it down and loading it onto flat cars, so that it could be re-established in the Urals, Siberia, Central Asia and the Caucasus. Hundreds of thousands of civilians made their own way east, whilst the vital factory workers were evacuated along with their equipment.

The stark reality of the first winter in Russia of 1941 to 1942 can be seen here. By the time Operation *Typhoon* was launched on 30 September, aiming to capture Moscow, time was already running out for the Germans, although they were still making huge inroads into Russian territory. The Germans made their last attempt to encircle the capital on 15 November. Twelve days later, elements of the 4th Panzer Army were just 19 miles from the Kremlin. By the beginning of December 1941, the Germans were beginning to suffer from lack of supplies and reinforcements, and the weather was taking its toll. It was at this stage, on 5 December, that Russian reinforcements, many transferred from the Far East and supported by T34s and rocket launchers, launched counterattacks against the Germans around Moscow. By 7 January 1942, the Germans were retreating from the capital.

The *Panzergrenadiers* examine a Russian BA10 armoured car in this photograph. This vehicle was introduced in 1938 and was built on the chassis of a GAZ truck. The superstructure was constructed from welded sheet steel and it had a 37mm gun and a ball-mounted machine gun in the turret. There was a second machine gun in the front hull plate.

An improved variant, the BA10M, was introduced in 1939, with a larger 45mm gun. The vehicles suffered from very poor off-road performance and this led to them being phased out. However, the BA10s did remain in service until 1942, by which time they had been converted into armoured personnel carriers. Enormous numbers of these half-tracked armoured cars were captured by the Germans and pressed into duty against partisans. The overall armour on the vehicle was 15mm; it had a road speed of 53km/h, dropping to 17km/h cross-country. In ideal circumstances, it had a range of 350km. It had a crew of four: a commander, a gunner, a loader and a driver.

Peeking inside another T34: the *Panzergrenadiers* do not seem content with having examined a number of these vehicles already and are possibly hoping to find some useful loot or food within the vehicle. In combat, the T34 initially suffered with some technical difficulties. It does not appear that this vehicle is damaged as such and it may have fallen foul of some of the problems that were common in the early stages. The transmission was prone to failing, the treads were relatively weak and the main and side clutches often failed. Sometimes, when they crossed ditches the tank's nose dug in due to its low profile. There was also an extreme shortage of experienced crews for the vehicle.

By December 1941, the Model 42 was introduced; it had better armour, a new five-speed gearbox, external fuel tanks to increase its range, a decreased number of parts to simplify production, wider tracks, a new gun cradle and a new cast turret. This was just one of the many improvements that the tank would go through over the course of the war. The last true T34/76 arrived in January 1943 and this time it had even better armour and a hexagonal-shaped cast turret, which was much easier to manufacture.

Chapter 3

An Infantryman's War

The German infantry division was undoubtedly the backbone of the German Army. They would never become fully mechanized or motorized. The German infantry would predominantly rely on horse-drawn transport and, in the war against Russia, would make great use of captured equipment.

The German infantryman was well trained and could make use of any weapon. They were not that reliant on external support, as they had their own heavy machine guns, mortars, anti-tank guns and artillery.

The German command structure at a tactical level was well integrated; it focused on combined arms. Senior non-commissioned officers and junior officers had a great deal of responsibility and invariably showed excellent initiative.

(Facing) This photograph shows a group of German infantry, fronted by an officer with a map case, resting before resuming their march. The German infantry uniform was of a practical and robust design. All of the men are wearing standard issue marching boots and the majority of them have attached their helmets to their waist belts. They seem to be invariably armed with rifles. The characteristic black leather 'y' strap webbing is clearly in evidence. There are two front straps, which hook to the 'd' ring on the back of the cartridge pouches. They would have an M31 haversack or bread bag, which was originally issued with a removable carrying strap. Regulations required them to carry it from their equipment belt. They also have entrenching tools, which were non-folding shovels. The men also have an M31 canteen, originally manufactured in aluminium.

This more casual shot clearly shows the men on campaign, as they are heavily equipped with all the essentials for fighting. Most of the men have K98 ammunition pouches. They were based on earlier designs, developed between 1909 and 1911. The men were issued with two of these pouches, each of which could carry thirty rounds of ammunition. All German personnel were also issued with a gas mask, carrying canister and accessories.

German infantry are on the march here. The man in the lead and others are wearing the Infantry Assault Badge. It is difficult to tell whether this is of the bronze or silver variety, therefore not assisting in identifying the exact nature of the unit. At this stage, MG34s would be issued to these units. The weapon was introduced in 1936 and it could be either magazine or belt fed, and could provide either light or heavy sustained fire. It was fitted with a bipod for light sustained fire, or a tripod for heavy sustained fire. It could fire up to 900 rounds a minute and it was fitted with a quick-change barrel to prevent overheating.

This is a group of captured Russian prisoners, making their way west, seemingly unguarded, while a mixed column of motorized and horse-drawn German transport continues east. The typical Russian infantry division of 1941 was under-equipped and poorly trained, and its paper strength rarely matched its actual strength. Many of the decent, experienced commanders had been purged in the late 1930s and political officers were attached to the units. Despite its enormous losses in 1941 and 1942, it managed to reinvent itself and become a far more effective fighting force. By the end of the war, the Russians boasted over 500 infantry divisions alone.

A pair of abandoned Russian guns; the one in the foreground appears to be a howitzer, while the other is an anti-tank weapon, possibly a 76mm divisional artillery gun, which could be used in an anti-tank role. We can also see an abandoned Komsomolets artillery tractor. These were originally introduced in 1934 to transport heavy artillery guns, crew and ammunition. The original was designed on the chassis of a T24 tank. It was used widely for transporting all kinds of field artillery. A lighter T20 was introduced in 1936, but the most common was the Voroshilovets, which was introduced in 1938. It had better transmission, running gear and winch.

A whole column of artillery tractors, ammunition carriers and artillery pieces have been abandoned here, to be captured by the Germans. These tractors appear to be the heavy tractor, Stalienez ChTZ S65 varieties. They were copies of US tractors, and fitted with diesel engines. Nearly 38,000 of these were built between 1937 and 1941. The principal reason behind the fact that this column has clearly been caught by the rapid German advance is that they could only muster 7km/hour on the road.

An abandoned Russian anti-tank gun and tractor are shown here alongside the road, as Germans advance. In the first six months of the war Russian anti-aircraft artillery was often forced to defend itself against German tanks. Anti-aircraft units would be used to repel dive-bomber attacks in the first phase of the engagement. Anti-aircraft guns would then be used to help drive off tanks. This particular weapon appears to be a Russian 37mm M1939 anti-aircraft gun, based on the Bofors design. Around 20,000 of these were produced and it had been developed from 1933, based on the 25mm M1933 Bofors gun.

These abandoned weapons appear to be 76.2mm Russian anti-aircraft guns, designated 7.62cm Flak M31(R) by the Germans. There were also 85mm variants of this weapon. Arguably, owing to the size of these weapons, they could be 85mm air defence guns, or 52Ks. They were adopted by the Russians in 1939 and throughout the course of the war were credited with shooting down over 4,000 German aircraft. For each kill, nearly 600 rounds were fired.

Searchlights were extensively used against night-time aircraft attacks. This is an abandoned Russian searchlight, being investigated by a German officer. In many cases the searchlights would be used in pairs. They would be positioned at a known distance apart from one another, so that by using triangulation the altitude of the enemy aircraft could be worked out. This would then enable the fuses on the anti-aircraft flak shells to be calibrated for maximum effect.

The searchlights also caused difficulties for bomb aimers, using optical bomb sights. Searchlights were also used for ground actions. In the Battle of Berlin in April 1945, over 140 Russian searchlights were directed against German positions along the Neisse River, with the aim of temporarily blinding them, although the attempt actually failed due to fog and the Russians suffered heavy losses, delaying their capture of the German capital.

This vehicle is a Russian BA20, which was developed in 1936 for use by reconnaissance, communication and headquarters units. It was based on a civilian car, which was a modified version of a Ford design. The superstructure was made of welded sheet steel. The vehicle had a 7.62mm machine gun on a cylindrical turret. This particular version appears to be a BA20M, which was an updated version that could accommodate a third crewman, who was the radio operator. The weight increased to 2.6 tons. The vehicle range was around 150km. Although production ended in 1941, the vehicle continued to be used for many more months. It was fitted with supposedly unbreakable tyres; they were filled with spongy rubber and the vehicle had strengthened rear axles.

This is the first of two shots of a bogged-down KV2, which appears to have tried to cross over a dried watercourse by using a flimsy wooden bridge. Back in December 1939, the KV1 entered service and was combat tested during the Russian–Finnish war. The conclusion was that there was a need for a heavier tank with a more powerful armament, so that it could tackle bunkers, pillboxes and fortifications. Engineers worked to fit a 152mm howitzer, originally the 1909/1930 version and later the 1938/1940 model. There is a fascinating account given by an element of the 6th Panzer Division when it encountered KV2s on 25 June 1941:

> Unfortunately, the Russian 52-ton heavy tanks showed that it [sic] was almost insensitive to hits from the 10.5cm. Several hits from a 15cm gun were ineffective and bounced off. However, continuous attacks by several Panzer IV managed to knock out a large number of tanks throughout the day.

Many of the KV2 tanks were lost because of breakdowns. A prime example was the Russian 41st Tank Division, which lost twenty-two KV2s out of their thirty-three vehicles. Seventeen of these had to be abandoned because they had broken down or run out of fuel and only five were destroyed by enemy action. The KV2, although intimidating, was cancelled in October 1941 after 334 of the vehicles had been produced. The vehicle had the same drawbacks as the KV1, but most KV2s lacked sufficient ammunition. This did not stop the Germans from being shocked at the sight of them and, usually, in combat only an 88mm gun could knock one out.

This is an abandoned KV1, which is distinctive as it has a mounting for a machine gun on the rear of the turret. It has broad tracks, which enabled it to wade through mud and snow. Undergraduate students in Leningrad began studying heavy tanks in October 1938. The military wanted a multi-turreted heavy tank, while designers preferred a single-turret vehicle. It was finally decided to press ahead with the KV1, the first model being sent to Moscow for approval. By May 1940, production targets were set at 200 per year, but the army was concerned that it still had many defects and it had not undergone proper trials. Quality would ultimately be sacrificed for quantity.

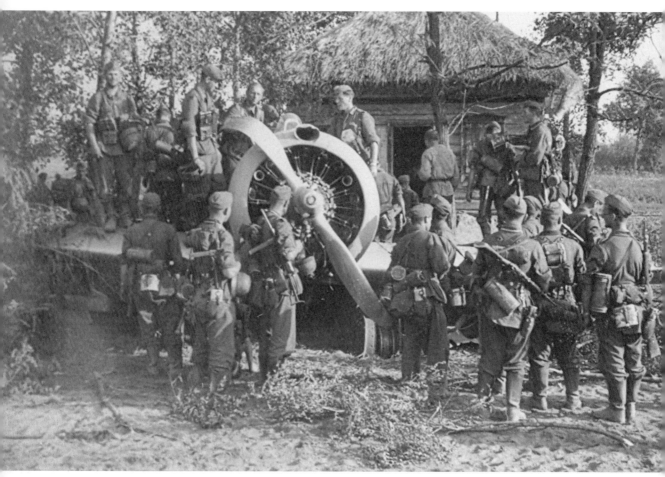

Although it is difficult to tell, because of the number of German soldiers investigating this downed Russian aircraft, it is likely to be an Polikarpov I-16. Production had begun in 1934 and it entered service in 1935. Many pilots found it difficult to fly and awkward to land and it became unpopular. Upgrades were introduced in 1937 and 1938 and it continued to improve. In 1939 under-wing racks were fitted to carry rockets, making it useful in a ground attack role. A better engine was also introduced, giving it an increase in speed to 411km/h and it also had a better rate of climb. The new version also had strengthened wing construction and in order to increase range had auxiliary fuel tanks. Although the production of the aircraft finished in March 1940, by Operation *Barbarossa* nearly half of the fighter aircraft were I-16s and it would remain in service until late-1943. The German pilots nicknamed it 'the rat' but the Russians preferred either 'hawk' or 'fly'.

This downed Russian aircraft appears to be an Ilyushin Il 4. Over 5,000 were produced between 1937 and 1944, the vast majority in the last three years. In many respects, the aircraft was the forgotten bomber of the war, even though it was the most numerous of Russian bombers. It performed to a reasonable standard, although the poor defensive armament meant that unacceptably high losses were suffered. The original design was first flown in 1935, and known as the TsKB-26. The production model was given the designation DB-3B (the 'DB' meaning 'long-range bomber') and first flown in 1940. Even against the Finns, the bombers were shot down in large numbers, a trend that would continue when Germany invaded.

A fantastic shot of a knocked out Russian armoured train. The Russians had a large number of armoured trains at the start of the war, but the vast majority of these were lost in 1941. The later trains were fitted with T34 or KV1 turrets, others with naval artillery guns. The main carriage behind the train itself is the Motorized Armoured Carriage MBV-2.

A pontoon bridge spans an unidentified Russian river, possibly the Dnepr. On 11 July 1941, Halder, head of the German OKH (*Oberkommando des Heeres*) wrote in his diary:

> The objective to shatter the bulk of the Russian Army this [western] side of the Dvina and Dnepr has been accomplished ... east of [these rivers] we would encounter nothing more than partial forces ... It is thus probably no overstatement to say that the Russian Campaign has been won in the space of two weeks.

The situation was not as clear cut as this as panzer general Heinz Guderian wrote:

> Since July 13th the Russians had been launching heavy counterattacks. Some twenty enemy divisions moved from the direction of Gomel against the right flank of my Panzer Group, while the Russians encircled in Mogilev and Orsha attempted simultaneously to break out, the former garrison in a south and south-easterly direction, the latter toward the south. All of these operations were controlled by Marshal Timoshenko, with the obvious objective of belatedly frustrating our successful crossing of the Dnepr.

German troops in rainproof capes. Essentially, this was a waterproof triangle manufactured in tightly woven cotton drill and issued to all men in the German Army. The *zeltbahn*, as it was called, was developed in 1931. The dimensions of the triangular shelter quarter are 250 × 200 × 200cm. Each side had a row of eleven aluminium, zinc or steel buttons used to connect two shelter quarters together. On the base there was one button, then a row of six buttons to connect together to form a tent out of four quarters (*viererzelt*). These could then be attached to create a house tent (*hauszelt*). In the middle of the cape there was a slit and a button for individual use as a poncho. The coming of the rainy season in Russia or *raputitsa* literally brought the *blitzkrieg* to a standstill. This gave the Russians the chance to fight the Germans on more equal terms.

This photograph is marked 'Donez (sic) winter 1941–1942'. This is a bunker built near the Donets River, which was reached by German forces in the south by around 5 December 1941. The cold was so extreme that the *ersatz* rubber wheels and tyres turned to a wood-like consistency. Mineral oils became thick and were useless for lubricating weapons and unprotected hands froze to metal parts of weapons and vehicles. General Guderian was told by his superiors that tank engines needed to be warmed up for twelve hours before attempting to get them on the move. The over-reliance on horses by the Germans caused difficulties too, with food in short supply for them. The Germans were so unprepared for the harsh winter that they took clothing off Russian bodies to keep themselves warm and were not averse to stealing the clothes of Russian prisoners of war.

German soldiers at work repairing and reinforcing a small bridge in the depths of winter. Back on 6 September 1941, Hitler had released *Führer* Directive No. 35:

> The initial operational successes against enemy forces between the Army Group South's and Centre's adjoining flanks and additional successes in encircling enemy forces in the Leningrad region, have created the prerequisites for conducting a decisive operation against Army Group Timoshenko, which is conducting unsuccessful offensive operations on Army Group Centre's front. It must be destroyed decisively before the onset of winter within the limited time indicated in existing orders ... To this end we must concentrate all of the efforts of ground and air forces earmarked for the operation, including those that can be freed up from the flanks and transferred in timely fashion.

However, through the most extreme of sacrifices, the Russian Army managed to halt the Germans and the most severe Russian winter in living memory brought a temporary end to the German advances. By early December, the Germans were overextended, poorly equipped for winter, lacked sufficient reserves and occupied unprepared positions. The Germans had lost some 830,000 men by December 1941; around 185,000 of this total had been killed.

This is a shot of a large column of German infantry advancing toward a Russian town in early 1942. The Germans' 1942 strategic summer offensive was a continuation of Operation *Barbarossa* and struck at southern Russia. It lasted from 28 June to 19 August. *Fall Blau* (Case Blue) as the operation was known, led to spectacular gains for the Germans. By 5 July, the leading units of the German 4th Panzer Army had reached the River Don and were assaulting the city of Voronezh. There was desperate Russian resistance and the Germans were pinned down long enough for the Russians to hastily patch up their defences elsewhere. Unlike in 1941, when the Germans finalized the encirclement of the city, the bulk of the Russian defenders had slipped away. The Germans believed that this was a sign that the Russians were down to their last reserves when, in fact, they had withdrawn in good order.

A German field car or light truck in Russia in early 1942. The vehicle appears to be a Krupp L 3 H 163. They were built in the period 1936–1938 and the overall production numbers amounted to some 2,000 (including L 3 H 63). It was a 6 × 4 military truck. The first lorry was developed by the Krupp AG, Essen, Abt. Kraftwagenfabrik Company and was manufactured in 1919. Before the beginning of the war, Krupp manufactured a large variety of different vehicles. Krupp would go on to produce light, medium and heavy transports for the German Army. One of the company's most famous vehicles was the Krupp Protze. It was a six-wheeled truck and artillery tractor powered by a 60hp Krupp M 304 four-cylinder engine. It was used for a variety of different purposes, including transporting personnel, towing artillery and other utility uses. The vehicle was used extensively in most theatres of the war. It was commonly nicknamed Boxer due to its simple design. Around 7,000 Boxers were produced from 1933 to 1942.

This is a German officer organizing a labour gang comprising captured Russian soldiers. The shoulder strap may indicate the German soldier in the foreground is, in fact, a sergeant major, although it is difficult to be precise. An enormous number of Russian prisoners of war were taken, particularly in the period 1941–1942. Many of them would not survive the war. An official justification used by the Germans for the harsh treatment of Russian prisoners was that Russia had not signed the Geneva Convention. The Germans determined that Russian prisoners taken during the campaign would not have the protection of international and customary law. Orders were issued to the effect that German military penal code and the Hague Convention would not apply. In March 1941 Hitler issued what would become known as the Commissar Order:

> [Operation *Barbarossa* was to be a conflict of] ideologies and racial differences and will have to be waged with unprecedented, unmerciful, and unrelenting hardness. Any German soldier who breaks international law will be pardoned. Russia did not take part in the Hague Convention and, therefore, has no rights under it.

These are Russian civilian males that have been taken into captivity for labour duties for the Germans. Russian civilian loses were enormous during the war. In the period 1941–1945 an estimated 7,420,379 were killed by the Germans as a result of military actions, including deliberate killings and reprisals. A further 2,164,313 died whilst engaged in forced labour in Germany and another 4,100,000 died as a direct result of the occupation, including starvation, disease and lack of medical care. From 1942 to 1945, around 1.4 million labourers were in the service of the Organization Todt. These were compulsory workers from occupied countries; effectively they were used as slave labourers.

German Army wagons being prepared. Note the stands of personal weapons and equipment to the rear. Some 80 per cent of the German transport was equestrian. Despite all the misconceptions about *blitzkrieg*, the impressive German technology and development, their design and production capabilities, the day to day reality was that on average some 1.1 million horses were being used. Even after the *blitzkrieg* period, in 1942, of the 322 German divisions, just fifty-two of them were armoured or motorized. According to the *Intelligence Bulletin*, March 1946:

> The old-type German infantry division had approximately 5,300 horses, 1,100 horse-drawn vehicles, 950 motor vehicles, and 430 motorcycles. In 1943, due to the great difficulties in supply and upkeep of motor vehicles in the wide stretches of the Eastern Front, the allotment to divisions in that theatre was reduced to approximately 400 motor vehicles and 400 motorcycles, and the number of horses was increased to some 6,300. The 1944-type divisions had about 4,600 horses, 1,400 horse-drawn vehicles, 600 motor vehicles, and 150 motorcycles.

A column of Russian prisoners of war trudge west to an uncertain future. At the head of the column there appears to be a number of Russian naval personnel. The usual dress of sailors when used as naval infantry was a short pea jacket (*bushlat*) and trousers tucked into boots, while retaining their sailor's cap (*bezkoziyrka*). Some of the naval infantry would wear their ordinary shipboard uniform with the pullover (*flanelevka*) that includes the square rig collar. When the Germans invaded in 1941, the size of the Russian Navy and Air Force was very small compared with the vast Red Army. Many of the naval vessels were bottled up in ports and, for the majority of the war, the navy was reduced to convoy protection and support for land-based operations. This meant that there was a sizeable pool of available manpower and many of the sailors served as infantry – they played a significant role in the defence of Leningrad and Moscow and were involved in amphibious operations in the Crimea.

This is the last shot of the collection showing a formed up column of German infantry led by what appears to be a German major. He is wearing the old-style *schirmmütze* or uniform cap. A variety of these were worn in differing styles and quality. Army officers below the rank of general all wore the same basic style and colouring of cap. The peak was shiny black with a slight ridge running along the edge. The insignia was in white metal.

Chapter Four

Flak and Artillery Collection

This small album of ten photographs focuses on the flak and artillery units that were deployed by the Germans in Operation *Barbarossa*.

In line with the German military doctrine of flexibility, effective German anti-aircraft units were integral parts of all military formations. Initially at least, they would be designated as either heavy, mixed or light, depending on the particular weapons that they were issued with and whether or not they used searchlights. While it might be expected that German anti-aircraft units were organic parts of the German Air Force, independent anti-aircraft units belonged to infantry, panzer and artillery units in the army.

Prior to the outbreak of the Second World War, the Germans tested various weapons and tactics during the Spanish Civil War. The campaign in Poland in 1939 gave them a chance to refine the mix of weapons and decide whether they should be standardized, along with the deployment of the weapons. It was clear to the Germans that they needed a weapon that could be used against both aircraft and mechanized ground vehicles. A valuable lesson from both Spain and Poland was that the anti-aircraft guns needed to be highly mobile. Prior to this, conventional wisdom had suggested that they should be static, particularly for protection against hostile aircraft.

The Germans had learned that they could use their anti-aircraft weapons in forward areas in an offensive role. This tactic was proven during the Polish and French campaigns and, later, in Libya. Anti-aircraft guns needed to have a high rate of fire; they needed rapid-fire control calculation, quick tracking speeds and high muzzle velocity. In effect, this made them ideal in an anti-tank role and, consequently, they needed a mobile carriage or mount to make them more mobile, but it needed to be strong enough to withstand the recoil of high elevation anti-aircraft fire, or horizontal fire.

The Germans divided their flak guns, as we have seen, into three general classifications. Light guns would tend to be 20mm; medium guns would include 37mm and 47mm whilst the heavier flak units would be 75mm, 88mm, 105mm and 150mm.

In the field, all German combat units were deemed to be responsible for their own anti-aircraft defence against low flying aircraft. Even rifle-armed men were trained to use it against aerial targets. They could provide protection up to around 500m.

Machine guns were also used, being effective up to about 800m. The light and medium-calibre anti-aircraft guns would engage from around 2,000m. The heavier anti-aircraft artillery could be used at distances of up to 9,000m.

A typical full-strength light anti-aircraft battery, confusingly often referred to as a company, would include around twelve light guns. A panzer division, for example, would have as many as three of these in addition to a heavy anti-aircraft battery, consisting of six heavy guns and two light guns. This is typical of a panzer division around May 1942.

This is a small German flak gun overlooking a shattered Russian town. The German Army used standard 2cm flak guns during this period of the war. During the early years of the war, both the Flak 30 and Flak 38 were used in all services, but were increasingly relegated to second-line service by 1941. The main problem with the design of the earlier weapons was the relatively slow rate of fire; around 120 rounds per minute design remained the fairly low rate of fire, which at 120rpm was not particularly fast for a weapon of this calibre.

This is a deployed German 20mm anti-tank weapon and its crew. Gun positions were carefully chosen; in their primary anti-aircraft role a battery of four heavy anti-aircraft guns would be positioned in a square approximately 700m across. They would tend to engage targets no more than around 2,000m away, even if they were 88mm weapons. This general rule would apply to engaging ground targets. Light and medium flak guns were normally deployed in platoons of three and usually in a triangular layout. The guns would often be positioned between 75m and 150m apart. It was comparatively rare for them to be deployed singly, but when being used for targeting ground units they could be deployed independently, usually reliant on the fields of fire that the particular gun position would offer.

An in-action shot, taken as a crewman sprints to safety while under artillery fire; note the hasty nature of the defensive positions and the fact that the artillery piece has been partially concealed. During the campaigns in France and in Poland the Germans had at least local aerial superiority, so they did not pay a great deal of attention to the camouflage of their anti-aircraft positions or guns. In Russia, they did not necessarily have definitive air superiority and consequently they did use camouflage and erected dummy gun positions in an attempt to deceive the enemy and assist in maintaining the secrecy of their actual deployment. A great deal of cunning and ingenuity was used. Vehicles as well as guns would be camouflaged with nets and foliage, and they would be dispersed as much as possible, allowing for the tactical circumstances. In many instances guns were not noticed until they opened fire.

An enemy shell lands perilously close to a German gun position in this photograph, which was taken shortly after the previous one and shows the dangers if the enemy has been able to zero in on static anti-aircraft positions. As far as the Germans were concerned, their fire power was organized to increase directly in proportion to the resistance that they encountered. In defence, a German commander would always try to find suitable ground where infantry, machine guns, anti-tank weapons, artillery and tanks would all be able to operate with the maximum efficiency. If time and resources allowed, defensive areas would be in-depth. The commander would usually construct defensive areas that were capable of all-round defence. This meant that the artillery would be positioned where it could support any part of the defensive area and the tanks would be positioned so that they could be used to launch counterattacks.

The coastal area of a Russian town burns in the distance, as a crewman of an anti-tank gun consults his maps. Active German anti-aircraft units would be responsible for observing the air, using specially trained personnel. The air guards, as they were often referred to, would submit detailed reports of hostile aircraft in the area. The battalion headquarters would then forward appropriate warnings up the chain of command. Anti-aircraft units would be allocated to protect installations, including depots, parks, railheads, bridges and airfields. The size of the force would be dependent on what was available and whether local air superiority had been achieved. The light and medium anti-aircraft guns were highly manoeuvrable and would engage a target immediately as it came into view and range. They would rely, for effect, on the high rate and volume of their fire. They were extremely accurate firing at aircraft at altitudes below 500m. At very low level, less than 15m to 20m, their accuracy would be considerably reduced; they would only have a split second to engage the target as it flashed by.

This photograph is of a downed Ilyushin DB3, a Russian bomber aircraft. It was a twin-engine, low-wing monoplane. Some 1,528 were built and the last production batches came out of the factories in 1940. The test flight of the prototype, the DSKB30, took place in 1936 and it was ordered into production in the August. It was a difficult aircraft to manufacture, as there were many rivets and numerous welds that had to be checked using x-ray machines. It was designed to carry ten 100kg bombs, but for short-range operations it could carry a total of 2,500kg of bombs on external bomb racks. It had a crew of three and for close protection it had three machine guns. Over the course of the period from 1937 to 1939 a number of improvements were made to the aircraft. The second stage of the upgraded version was known as the DB3B.

One of the most famous operations launched by these aircraft belonged to the torpedo-bomber variant, DB3T, from the Russian Baltic Fleet. They dropped the first Russian bombs on Berlin on 8 August 1941; fifteen aircraft were involved in the mission. There is only one known surviving example, which is at the Central Museum of the Air Forces in Monino, to the east of Moscow. This aircraft was recovered from a forested area in September 1988 and restored for display.

A German soldier is in a trench on sentry duty in this photograph. Note the two German grenades, or *stielgranate*, alongside the soldier's rifle. This is a characteristic German stick grenade weapon, often referred to as the 'potato masher', which was adopted by the Germans back in 1924. It was officially a Model 24; a friction lighter was used to ignite the charge. There was a pull cord that ran down the hollow handle from the detonator and this was held in place by a detachable cap around the base of the stick. The soldier would remove the base cap by unscrewing it, which would let a porcelain ball and cord fall out. He would then pull the cord, which would drag a rough, steel rod through the igniter, causing it to flare. A five-second fuse would then begin to burn.

The grenade could be thrown up to 40m and the design reduced the risk of it rolling back towards the thrower in difficult terrain. They were used primarily against infantry positions, but were not that useful against armoured vehicles. For these, the grenades would be put into a bundle with six heads without their sticks, all wired up to the central stick grenade.

This appears to be a knocked out or abandoned Russian BT7 tank. BT, or Bystrokhodny Tanks, or 'fast tanks', were direct ancestors of the T34. The BT series of tanks was brought into production in the early 1930s. This particular variety, the BT7, was the most numerous, with around 4,965 vehicles produced. They were used in large numbers in 1941 and many of them were either abandoned or destroyed and only a few remained operational in 1942. Nonetheless, a large number of these tanks were used as late as August 1945 when the Russians invaded Japanese-occupied Manchuria.

The BT7 Model 1935 had a welded hull and a 45mm gun, as well as a coaxial gun. There was a new version, the Model 1937, with a different turret and sloping armour. The Russians also produced a command version, an artillery support version with a howitzer, and the OP7, which was a flame-thrower version. It had a road speed of 85km/hour and a road range of 250km. In more difficult terrain its range was reduced to 120km. They were comparatively thinly armoured and therefore vulnerable to 20mm and 37mm guns. When the German invasion began the Russian Army was in the process of replacing the BT tanks with the T34.

This is a collection of captured Russian Maxim guns. Officially, this was the PM M1910, which literally meant that it was a Maxim gun that was on a Sokolov mount. The Maxim gun was the first self-powered machine gun, developed by Sir Hiram Maxim back in 1884. This weapon had been used by the Russian Army during the First World War and had been converted to use standard Russian rifle cartridges. It was a cumbersome, wheel-mounted weapon with a gun shield. By 1943, the Russians had begun to replace it with the SG43 Goryunov, a medium machine gun that could be mounted on vehicles and tripods.

The PM M1910 heavy machine gun had a rate of fire of around sixty shots per minute. With the shield it weighed 64.3kg and was fed by a 250-round belt. It was a solid and reliable weapon that was water-cooled and it remained in service until the early 1950s. The Russians made it under licence between 1905 and 1950 and it had been adopted by the Russian Army, using a corrugated jacket, very similar to the one used on the Vickers machine gun in 1910.

A return to the German sentry in his slit trench is shown here. The soldier seems to be wearing a German Army anorak, or *windblusen*. Some of these were officially issued and designed, while others were simply of civilian origin. They were pull-on jackets with pockets arranged at the front. They had a drawstring waist and had a reinforced button positioned in the centre of the jacket's skirt, allowing a tail piece to be buttoned up. The sleeves were elasticized at the wrist and there was an attached drawstring hood. At this stage of the war they were not camouflaged. They could be worn on the outside or tucked into the wearer's trousers. They were worn over the field service uniform tunic and not worn as a separate coat.

Chapter 5

Towards the First Winter

This is a collection of just over fifty photographs belonging to another unnamed German soldier, operating in Russia in 1941 to 1942. The collection incorporates what are clearly combat scenes, along with some rather more relaxed behind-the-front line scenes and, finally, a selection of photographs that chronicle the experiences of the first bitter winter in Russia for the German Army.

Although the five months from 22 June to 26 November 1941 had seen 187 Germans killed or posted missing, the wounded total had reached 555,000. Around two-thirds of these men would later return to duty. Over the first winter period on the Eastern Front, between 27 November and 31 March 1942, 108,000 were killed or missing and 268,000 were wounded. In addition, there were 228,000 frost-bite cases and over 250,000 suffering from typhus, diphtheria, stomach ailments, exhaustion, exposure, scarlet fever, and jaundice and skin problems. In fact, by April 1942 the Germans operating on the Eastern Front were at least 625,000 men under strength.

Approximately 250,000 horses had died that winter, and around 2,300 armoured vehicles had been lost by the Germans, of which around 1,600 were Panzer IIIs, Panzer IVs or assault guns. Losses elsewhere in weaponry saw the Germans at least 7,000 anti-tank guns short and 2,000 guns and howitzers under strength.

Although in this album we will see smiling Russian civilian faces, the early Russian counteroffensives had revealed the brutal character of the German occupation. Thousands of young men and women had been deported to Germany to be used as slave labourers. There had been indiscriminate massacres and many fine Russian towns and cities had been virtually levelled.

This is the first photograph of the collection and it may well be of a pre-war German transport column. The man in the foreground is wearing a Model 1938 field service cap (*feldmütze*). It was in field grey cloth with a small, inverted chevron of Russian braid. The cap also had a national emblem in cloth on the front of the upper part of the field cap. Although the sides were designed to be pulled down to be worn over the ears, this was seldom done. The sides of the cap were scalloped so that when worn in this manner there was still clear vision. It was also designed to be worn under a steel helmet.

This is an SdKfz232 eight-wheeled heavy armoured car, with the characteristically framed radio aerial over the superstructure. It was armed with an MG34 and a 20mm gun in the turret. The large frame aerial was quite cumbersome and vulnerable, and later models had a star-shaped aerial fitted to the rear decking. This armoured car had a range of around 300km and a maximum road speed of up to 85km/hour. The eight-wheeled version was produced between 1938 and 1943 but was to be superseded by the SdKfz234/2, or Puma. The SdKfz232 was not withdrawn from service, but was simply upgraded with better radio communication equipment. Originally, it was designed as a cavalry vehicle, but it proved to be ideal in a reconnaissance role, scouting ahead of heavier armoured formations. These vehicles were used against Poland and France and were also used initially in Russia and in North Africa. But the conditions would prove to be too severe for the vehicle. In the first wet season of the campaign in Russia in 1941, over 150 of the vehicles were immobilized due to the mud.

Maintenance work is seen here on a German Army field car. An enormous number of different manufacturers provided field or staff cars for the German Army, including Porsche and Mercedes-Benz. Certainly in the early stages of the war, the vehicles used were essentially military versions of civilian designs. In often extreme circumstances, many of these vehicles proved to be unsuited, and it was therefore inevitable that specific vehicles, such as the Kübelwagen, would not only be developed but also widely used by most units wherever possible.

A second shot of the early war column in this photo. These men appear to be wearing Model 1936 single-breasted tunics that were manufactured from a wool and rayon mixture, in field grey. They had five field grey metal buttons positioned down the front, with another button to each of the four, three-pointed pocket flaps. This was a style of pocket that was very similar to those worn during the First World War by the Austro-Hungarian Army.

The photograph here is clearly taken during the throes of the first Russian winter, in 1941/early 1942. The soldiers are now wearing the slightly later Model 1942 version of the field service cap. The truck appears to be a standard Opel Blitz, which was the backbone transport lorry for the Germans in the Second World War. This was one of the most common German trucks, which came into service in the 1930s. Over 100,000 of them were built and many were modified to become radio cars, buses and fuel trucks and others would have anti-aircraft guns mounted on them. Although it was a light truck, it could carry a considerable amount of weight. It had a very reliable six-cylinder engine and would prove to be one of the toughest and most reliable vehicles of the war.

This is a German bus with a three-man crew taking a break and posing for the camera. There were a number of versions of the Opel Blitz, which were used as buses, including the 3-ton, the Opel Blitz 3.6-ton, the 2.5-ton and the 1-ton. The Opel Blitz 3.6-ton was a thirty-seater bus and produced from 1939. Production finished in 1944, by which time nearly 3,000 of them had been constructed. There were dozens of different omnibuses that were used by the German Army based on commercial chassis of German and foreign manufacturers. Many of the earlier buses were actually open-topped, which betrayed their civilian roots.

This photograph is slightly damaged, but shows a posed scene of the men of the unit without their field equipment. When these field service uniforms, Model M1936, were worn the top button and the collar hooks were allowed to remain undone. However, when troops returned to Germany on leave they were warned that the field blouse had to be buttoned up and the neck band worn. Patrols enforced this order.

The trousers that were worn were normally field grey in colour, straight legged and fairly high waisted. The trousers had four fly buttons and a top waist button and there were three sets of two buttons stitched to the outside of the waistband. One set of buttons was on either side of the front and one set at the back were for the braces. At the back of the trousers, in the waistband, there was a 'v' cut in that had a small, cloth half belt that could be joined with a small metal buckle. The trousers had two slanting side pockets. Sometimes the pockets would have flaps. With or without, they all had one button to each pocket opening or pocket flap. There was a small fob pocket on the right-hand side of the front of the trousers and also a metal ring stitched to the outside of the waistband (sometimes a small, cloth loop), which was designed to secure the pocket watch chain. There was another pocket at the rear of the trousers, on the right hip, and in most cases it did not have a flap but was simply secured by a button.

The men are also wearing standard German Army black leather marching boots. On other occasions short ankle boots could be used.

A close-up of one of the soldiers from the previous group can be seen in this photograph. The man has his German Army aluminium belt buckle clearly in view. The buckle itself was rectangular in shape and had the words in German 'God with us'. In the centre was a German eagle and swastika. There was an enormous variety of different belt buckles, but the majority had two spikes at the back to secure the buckle to the belt. On some of the buckles there was a manufacturer's mark and they would usually be painted in green. It has been estimated that there were around a hundred different types developed; some of the originals were made from steel.

Two German soldiers stand guard in an improvised defensive position here. The men are both wearing their full kit, with all of their personal equipment. The bulk of the equipment was attached to the so-called 'y' straps. They were secured to both the front and rear of the belt and were used to carry mess tins, bread bags, and gas-mask canisters. The soldiers would also have had short handle, folding trench tools. Both of the men are armed with KAR98K rifles, which had five rounds in the magazine.

A pair of what appears to be Russian officers, or political commissars, feature in this photograph. Introduced after the Russian Civil War (1917–1921), commissars were brought in to watch over professional officers. Commissars had to give their approval to any major order. They were selected for their loyalty to the Communist Party. In theory, they were responsible for political indoctrination, training and morale, but many of them interfered with military matters. There had been officer purges in the 1930s, where officers had been criticized and denounced and many liquidated. This meant that the Russian Army was lacking in experienced officers and leadership was incompetent, or at best the officers had been cowed into submission by the commissars.

A typical German soldier, with all of his personal equipment, and the characteristic map case hanging on his right hip from his belt can be seen in this photo. He stands next to an officer with binoculars. These binoculars were black, either in a leather or Bakelite case, which would be hung on the right hip. Most of them were standard 6 × 30 binoculars and they would have a three-letter code, which was engraved on the binoculars to identify the factory in which they had been made.

German infantry take a rest between operations. The infantryman sitting to the left of the photograph has an MP40 machine pistol, which had an eight-round magazine. Most of the men, however, would be armed with the KAR98K, the standard bolt-action rifle that had been first produced in Belgium in 1924. It had a ten-year production life from 1935. A trained soldier could fire fifteen rounds per minute, but it only had a five-round magazine, so it was not ideal in a fire fight. It was a 7.92mm weapon with a maximum effective range of some 800m.

This is a deployed German MG34. The Germans did not produce separate heavy and light machine gun designs; instead they preferred dual-purpose weapons that could be fired either on a tripod or, as in this instance, on a bipod. This weapon had metal link belts of 250 rounds made up of fifty-round units. It was perfectly capable of providing sustained support fire, was relatively light and manoeuvrable and, above all, it was reliable.

The barrel was designed to be easily replaced, in order to avoid overheating, and changing the barrel was a simple matter. A latch would simply be disengaged, which held the receiver to the barrel sleeve. The receiver would then pivot to the right and the gunner could pull the barrel out of the sleeve. A new barrel could then be put inside the sleeve and the receiver rotated it back and latched. An experienced man could do this in a matter of seconds.

The weapon had a double trigger, which provided a select-fire capability. By pressing the upper segment of the trigger, the gun could fire on a semi-automatic rate and holding the lower segment of the trigger enabled the gun to be fully automatic. Although this was a considerable innovation, it was complex and did not appear in the successor weapon, the MG42. Used with a bipod, the weapon only weighed 12.1 kg.

A Russian BT tank, which has come to grief in a large shell hole and is now being inspected by curious German infantry, can be seen here. The majority of the large production BT tanks had 45mm tank guns. Between 1935 and 1940, some 5,328 BT7 tanks, excluding the BT7A of which 154 were made, were manufactured. It was designed to be a fast, long-range, tracked vehicle and it was a considerable improvement on the BT5, but clearly based on that design. It had a four-speed gearbox, headlights, an increased amount of ammunition on board and a better chassis. The BT7A was an artillery version that had a short-barrelled 76.2mm gun. A last attempt to modernize the BT7 took place prior to the German invasion, with the BT7M, with slightly better armour.

The legendary German 88mm Flak gun can be seen in this photograph. It is deployed but not crewed. Note the second weapon in the background. The Germans discovered that one of their heaviest flak guns was deadly in an anti-tank role. The 88mm would become a respected but feared weapon on every front. The version seen here is in its mobile guise on its tractor. The normal anti-aircraft position would be to demount it from the tractor and to extend the cruciform support legs. It was capable of firing around eight rounds per minute with a well trained crew of six. It could engage targets at well over 10,000m.

This is an interesting combat photograph, which shows the rigours of the fast-moving combat along the Russian front. Here, a messenger delivers information to a German officer in a field car. Note the man standing to the rear of the vehicle, who has radio equipment. Also note the German rifles in easy-to-reach positions close to the driver and the radio operator.

It is likely that the radio in operation was the Torn Fu, which was developed by Lorenz in the mid-1930s. It had a total weight, along with its accessory box, of 20kg. At this stage of the war this is likely to be the Torn Fu B1, which was actually introduced in 1936. It had a limited range and could be carried as a pack set by two men: one carrying the transceiver and the other the battery pack, which also housed the key, headphones, microphone, antennae gear and other accessories.

An MG34 mounted on a tripod. Note that the soldier in the foreground is using a range finder. These were much smaller than the artillery range finders, but ideal for not only pinpointing targets for the machine gun, but also for close and long-range artillery support.

A pair of Russian M1910 Maxim guns with their deceased crewmembers, in a hastily dug defensive position on a Russian plain. An enormous number of these weapons were captured by the Germans but they tended not to use them due to their weight. They were, indeed, heavy and unwieldy, but extremely reliable. They had proven their worth during the First World War and this largely explains why they remained in production and in service until they gradually began to be replaced by their successor in 1943. These weapons had a muzzle velocity of 740m per second. The Maxim was also copied by the Finnish Army and used throughout the war. The gun was normally mounted on the two-wheeled Sokolov mount, as can be seen in this photograph. Theoretically, this meant that it was easier to manoeuvre and it dispensed with having to mount and dismount to rapidly move the heavy machine gun.

German infantry take up defensive positions in the corner of a field using the cover of the hedgerows for protection. Arguably one of the most significant reasons for the German failure to take the Russian capital Moscow, was the appointment of General Zhukov on 10 October 1941. He took over command of the West Front and along with it the defence of Moscow itself. Along his 174-mile front line, centring on Mozhaisk, some 62 miles to the west of Moscow, he had eight armies.

To some extent, Zhukov was aided by Hitler's own dithering. By mid-October it seemed certain that the capital would fall; martial law had been declared and the streets and prisons of the city were scoured for any semi-able-bodied man or better that could carry a weapon. Already, Stalin had ordered that many of the factories in and around Moscow were to be dismantled and to be moved hundreds of kilometres east. Yet Hitler determined that his forces should not push toward Moscow directly; they were to encircle it. By 18 October the German 9th Army had penetrated the outer defence lines of Moscow. Hundreds of thousands of Russian prisoners were still being scooped up.

A burning BA6 Russian armoured car is shown here. This was based on a domestic three-axle vehicle and was broadly based on the BA3, which itself had been a development of the original three-axle armoured car, the BA1. The BA6 weighed around 5.12 tons and between 1936 and 1938 the Izhorskij factory produced 386 of these vehicles. A track could be placed over the rear sets of wheels to give it better cross-country capability. Hydraulic jacks could be mounted to the front and rear to allow railway wheels to be fitted; they would be installed over the tyres and this took just thirty minutes. The turret was welded and was, in fact, the same turret as the T26 light tank.

This is the first of two photographs featuring the 10.5cm le FH 18 light field howitzer. This was the standard weapon used by the German Army. It had been developed in the late 1920s and entered service in the mid-1930s. It had either wooden spoke or pressed steel wheels; the former were used when the weapon was being pulled by horse transport. It was not initially fitted with a muzzle brake but these were fitted from 1941, giving it a longer range. The weapon weighed 1,985kg and was normally operated by a crew of five. It had an effective range of approximately 11,000m.

The gun tube was of monoblock construction, with a counter recoil cylinder above it. The elevating mechanism allowed the weapon to be used either as a direct fire weapon or as a howitzer. The long tube allowed a high muzzle velocity and the long split trail made it stable when used as a direct fire weapon. The breech mechanism slid horizontally and was simply designed. There were built-in safety devices to allow the firing mechanism only to work when the breech block was either in the fully open or fully closed position. In the foreground we can see some of the ammunition. They used standard high-explosive shells, consisting of a shell case, a primer, a propelling charge of nitro-glycerine powder, and a quick percussion fuse, or, alternatively, a time and percussion fuse could be used.

This German soldier is using a battery commander's telescope. This was a ten-power binocular instrument that was used for observation and it also measured azimuths and angles of sight. The instrument consisted of a telescope and an azimuth mount, tripod, carrying case and accessories. There was also a trench mount, which could be embedded into the ground instead of using the tripod. The telescope arms could be positioned vertically, as in the picture, or swung horizontally in order to increase the stereoscopic effect. To set up the instrument the tripod legs were clamped at the desired length and embedded into the ground. To prepare the telescope, the clamping knob was released and the telescope arms turned to either the vertical or horizontal position. If required, light or dark filters could be put over the eye pieces.

This photograph appears to show a completely wrecked Russian KV1 tank. These were named after the Russian defence commissar and politician, Kliment Voroshilov. By comparison, they had fairly heavy armoured protection and when Operation *Barbarossa* got underway around 500 of the 22,000 tanks available to the Russian Army were KV1s. At 45 tons they were twice as heavy as most of the German tank opposition that they would encounter. By 1942, the KV1 was no longer as invincible as before, as the Germans were deploying longer-barrelled 50mm and 75mm guns.

This shot is of an abandoned Russian 122mm howitzer, towed by a slow-moving artillery tractor. The tractor looks to be a YA12. The Russians had adopted the 122mm gun in 1936 and the main production weapon was the M1931, of which around 2,450 were produced. An enormous amount of Russian artillery was lost in the early months of the war in Russia. The Germans used over 400 of the captured weapons and even manufactured their own ammunition for them. As the war developed, there were other versions of the 122mm gun, notably the ISU122 assault gun, which was perfectly capable of taking on and beating German tanks at extreme ranges.

This photograph appears to feature a First World War vintage 122mm howitzer, or M1910/30. Only production statistics for this weapon exist between 1937 and 1941, when production ceased. By this stage, 3,395 new pieces had been produced and over 760 old M1910 guns had been upgraded. The weapon was a typical short-barrelled howitzer. The object to the rear of the seated German officer is a gun caisson, which would have contained the ammunition. The weapon had a limited towing speed, as it had unsprung wheels. It also had limited elevation and traverse. It had a considerably shorter range than the German 10.5cm le FH 16; however, it was rugged and fairly reliable and well liked by the Russian Army.

An artillery crew are building a communication or defensive bunker in this photograph, on the reverse of a slope in Russia. The bunkers were shallow, scooped-out emplacements, usually surrounded by stone or earth walls. They were covered with packed earth or riveted stone to a height of 3 or 4 feet. As can be seen in the photograph, the roofs were reinforced by heavy timbers. This bunker appears to be a shelter, rather than an emplacement as such, and may only have been intended to have a single exit. In fact, even front-line German bunkers had few riflemen in them; the men were held back and only a handful of men were used in forward listening posts. This meant that forward defensive works tended to only have machine guns. When an enemy attack came, mortars and artillery could be brought down on the attacking force and the riflemen used to counterattack. The idea with the bunkers was to blend them in with the general terrain and make them almost indistinguishable until the enemy was very close.

A mounted German artilleryman features in this photograph. We have seen that the Germans had a heavy reliance on horses throughout the war. It was no different for artillery units, whose guns tended to be drawn by six horses. Scouts, observers and battery commanders would also favour, where possible, the opportunity to investigate on horseback the local terrain and to spot likely areas of approach by the enemy. A typical horse-drawn battery would have 105mm guns or 150mm howitzers drawn by six horses. The battalion commander would be mounted, as would the signal platoon and possibly the survey section.

Friendly German soldiers posing with local Russian peasants appear in this image. At least in the beginning, the regular German Army forces had fairly reasonable relations with Russian civilians. But many German soldiers regarded the Russians, being communist, as inherently treacherous. As the war on the Eastern Front ground on, these attitudes were reinforced and atrocities resulted. Brutality and murder would serve to alienate potential allies, generate resistance and contribute to the way in which German soldiers would ultimately be treated when they fell into Russian hands.

A well-disguised German bunker, or dugout, on the edge of a field is seen here. Every attempt has been made to conceal this bunker and the German soldiers would have regularly replaced the cut vegetation on the top of the roof, in order to avoid telltale signs of excavation. Bunkers such as these are still being found in Russia and there is a lively trade in the artefacts that have been found inside, including wartime coins, can and bottle openers, harmonicas, pocket knives and various items of personal military equipment.

A close-up of a German soldier, in his Model 1936 service tunic. The shoulder straps were of dark blue/green material, which was normally removable from the tunic. The tunic itself was slightly waisted, giving a slight flare to the skirt. There was a small inner pocket located on the inside lower edge to the right-hand side flap of the tunic front. This was designed to hold a standard issue field dressing pack. The tunic had a deep vent in the centre rear. The sleeves were without cuff turn-backs and were split so that the sleeve ends could be wrapped tighter around the wrist and then buttoned into position. The neckband was removable and worn inside the collar of the tunic and attached using three small metal collar studs.

A group of captured Russian soldiers with their German captors can be seen here in a small Russian village. Underneath the greatcoat the Russian rifleman would wear a *gymnastiorka* jacket, with reinforced elbows. He would also wear khaki *sharovari* trousers, with puttees and low black boots and would normally be armed with the standard Moisin Model 1891 infantry rifle. It appears from this photograph that the men are, in fact, wearing black leather boots and normal trousers.

Here we see German units on the move across a Russian plain, while the remnants of a Russian defensive position blazes in the distances. Even from the very beginning German troops were not averse to taking as much food and other items as they could carry. This often condemned the civilians to a slow death by starvation. Initially, guerrilla resistance in 1941 was limited to pockets of bypassed Russian soldiers. This was understandable since in just the first three weeks of the war German troops had penetrated 360 miles into Russian territory. The ferocity of the Russian resistance came as a great surprise to the Germans and even though enormous amounts of territory had been taken and would continue to be taken, the German Army was well behind its offensive timetable. German commanders were also worried that intelligence sources were not accurately predicting concentrations of Russian troops, their deployment and their strength.

A group of German soldiers cross a Russian river with their bicycles in an inflatable boat here. Germans would often use several inflatable boats to create light assault bridges, which consisted of prepared wooden sections. Bridges could be constructed up to 80 feet long. The individual timber frames were lashed to the inflatable boats. A single section could be carried and assembled by two men.

A photograph perhaps taken a minute or so too soon, as the German soldier in the centre is still combing his hair in preparation for the shot. Most of the men seem to be carrying their entrenching tools. These were known as *kleines schanzzeug*, which literally means 'small entrenching tool'. It was effectively unchanged since the 1880s and the overall length was around 55cm. The blade was 14.5cm wide and 18.5cm long. The blade itself was riveted to an unpainted, wooden handle. In many cases, the German soldiers would have filed off the rivets to avoid catching their hands while using the tool. The blades were often stamped with a manufacturer's code and they would also have the date and an 'H', signifying *Heer*, or army. The carrier for the tool was made of leather, with a rim at the front. The tool was secured to the carrier with a leather strap, which then wrapped around the handle. There would also be belt loops sewn between the back piece and the rim so that it could be suspended from the belt of the soldier. Until around 1938 the carriers were made of leather, but after this they were often made of artificial leather and later war models were made of black or tan pressed cardboard.

This is a familiar face in the photographs, showing a German *gefreiter*. In this photograph we can clearly see the ammunition pouches, which were introduced to the German Army in 1909. However, the majority of the Second World War issue pouches were of the 1911 type. The difference between the two was that the 1909 pouch could carry forty-five rounds and the 1911 just thirty.

The pouches were made up of three compartments, each one carrying two five-round clips. Each soldier was given two such pouches, giving him a total of sixty rounds. There was a divider in each of the pouches to separate the two clips of ammunition. The pouches were either brown or black pebbled leather, although there were some smooth leather ones. Sometimes brown leather pouches were actually painted black and, in fact, in July 1943 an order was issued that all brown pouches had to be painted black. Regulations dictated that the pouches were to be worn some 3cm from the belt buckle. The pouches made in the 1930s and in the early war years were stitched. Later pouches were riveted.

German troops, vehicles and equipment sprint across a bridge in Russia in this image. Although captured bridges would have been checked for mines and explosives, it was highly probable that the precise coordinates of the bridge had been noted by retreating Russian forces. This photograph suggests that the bridge crossing is taking place quite close to the front line, which would mean that if the German force had been spotted then the Russians were likely to bring down artillery fire on and around the bridge itself.

German troops pause for a break to grab food and have a short rest before moving on. Most of the men are wearing German Army greatcoats and we can clearly see all of their personal equipment hanging from either their 'y' strap or belt. Some of the seated individuals to the left of the photograph are wearing ponchos.

Of particular note is the M31 bread bag, which was a simple, single compartment haversack that contained the men's rations. The bread bags dated from around 1932 and were still in production until at least 1944. The early examples had aluminium hardware, but post-1939 production began to change and zinc and steel were used instead. In many of the later versions leather tabs were dispensed with, as were the leather reinforcements. The early war types were in field grey but by 1941 some of the bread bags were olive green. There were belt loops and a hook to secure the bread bag to the belt. Some early war examples had greenish paint on the leather. Underneath the belt loops were 'd' rings, which would be used to hold the field bottle on the right and the mess tin on the left. There were also leather tabs that were used to secure the field bottle and mess tin straps, to prevent them from bouncing around when the soldier was running.

This is a photograph of a Russian goods train in winter, which was probably taken in the early months of 1942. Note on the right-hand side the very basic barrier to prevent road traffic from crossing the line. Initially, the *Luftwaffe* was tasked with destroying Russian railways and it was proposed that parachute or airborne troops be used to capture railway bridges. But this was entirely dependent on air superiority.

A long column of German armour proceeds along a Russian road, while slower moving, horse-drawn transport is relegated to the side of the road. This photograph was also taken during the early winter months of the campaign.

These German soldiers are presumably negotiating the sale rather than the theft of livestock with Russian peasants. The sheer rapidity of the German advance far outstretched the army's ability to feed and to re-provision or re-arm their men. Comparatively speaking, the German soldiers were poorly equipped for the winter months and would have to scavenge for food and take clothes from prisoners of war.

Another photograph that was taken in the first few weeks of German occupation can be seen here. In many parts of Russia, the Germans were initially welcomed, not so much as conquerors, but as liberators. Russia consisted of a huge variety of different ethnic groups, many of which had independence aspirations and felt no particular allegiance to Moscow or to communism.

This photograph shows the stark realities of the first winter on the front in 1941. This German soldier is wearing an eye patch to protect a wound, yet he is still operating in severe winter conditions. *Führer Directive No. 39*, dated 8 December 1941, recognized the problems of the early onset of winter on the Eastern Front and with it re-supply difficulties and the requirement to cease large-scale offensive operations. The directive ordered that the German Army was to hold onto regions that had particular operational or economic importance, to rest and replenish units and to create a situation where the men would be ready to resume large-scale offensive operations in the following year.

German soldiers are using Russian civilian horse-drawn sledges here to carry out patrols. During the winter of 1941 to 1942, most of the German mechanized units were effectively immobilized. The German Army relied on horses and, to some extent, ski units. Even as early as July 1941 it was clear that the German Army was running short of boots and already staff officers were thinking about clothing requirements for winter. By the time the winter did strike, the German army lacked reserves and they occupied unprepared positions. The Russians used this to their advantage, concentrating on key points where they could obtain temporary superiority in numbers.

This is a German officer, wearing an animal skin fur coat. Many wore German Army greatcoats lined with fur, although these were in relatively short supply. It quickly became apparent that woollen balaclavas, extra thick woollen underwear, sweaters, mittens, double-breasted guard coats, felt over-shoes and a host of other clothing, including sheepskin overcoats, quilted jackets and trousers and leather-reinforced, felt, calf-length boots, were all needed for the winter months on the Eastern Front. Unfortunately for the men, these were often a long time coming.

German officers consider their options, as an artillery observer uses a binocular periscope to survey the surrounding countryside. The insignia on the staff car seems to imply that this is part of the 162nd Infantry Division, which operated on the Eastern Front between June 1941 and April 1942. The 162nd would later be the home of the Turkistan Legion, which was formed in the spring of 1942. In its new guise it would see extensive action in Yugoslavia and Italy. Many of the native Turcoman troops would be repatriated to Russia after the war was over, to a far from certain future. The German 162nd was actually disbanded in Poland and the staff were charged with raising and training six eastern legions. They eventually raised and trained eighty-two battalions.

This is a good view of the preparedness required when visiting the front line. Note the number of rifles strapped into position within the staff car, as the officers discuss tactics in front of the vehicle.

A line of predominantly horse-drawn transports feature in this photograph, which have been drawn up with supplies and fodder. A number of motorized transport vehicles are braving the mud, whilst the rest of the wagons are dispersed around the area, to avoid casualties should the area come under artillery fire.

This is an abandoned Russian howitzer and its tractor, which appears to have been burned out. The vehicle in the centre appears to be an ammunition caisson. It was not just equipment that the Russian Army was losing in the period of German ascendancy on the Eastern Front; according to official records the Russians lost 1,656,517 men across the entire front. Around 636,383 of these had been killed, captured or were missing. This estimated figure is considered to be on the low side and the total losses, until the end of 1941, were expected to be something in the region of two million. These were catastrophic losses. In all, the Russians had lost 2.8 million in the first three months and another 2 million from October to December.

This is a vast T35 multi-turreted heavy Russian tank. It had a short 76.2mm gun, two 45mm high-velocity guns and a pair of machine guns for close defence. It was based on the Vickers Independent Tank of the early 1930s and it had a crew of ten and weighed 45 tons. The main problem was that it only had up to 30mm of armour.

A German artillery gun and crew; note the large stocks of ammunition to the rear and the fact that the crew seem to have a reasonable expectation of not coming under fire, as no precautions have been taken to hide their position or to place the ammunition at a safe distance. Also note the wooden crates of ammunition to the left of the picture.

The gun crew and support team are posing beside their howitzer here. The men seem to have made an effort with their uniforms and we can presume that this was at the successful end of a particular operation. Even by December 1941 there were an estimated 1.7 million Germans on the Eastern Front, with 1,170 tanks, 615 aircraft and 13,500 artillery pieces. But this was according to official Russian figures and, in fact, there were 240,000 Germans with 600 tanks and 5,350 artillery pieces.

Chronology of Operation *Barbarossa* (June–December 1941)

Date	Event
22 June	Operation launched – good progress in north and centre. Stiff resistance in the south.
24 June	Pockets sealed off at Bialystok, Novogrudok, and Volkovysk.
26 June	Brest Litovsk falls. In the north the Germans enter Daugavpils.
1 July	Germans cross the River Berezina and the River Divna and advance on Pskov.
4 July	Germans capture Ostrov.
9 July	Minsk pocket reduced and Germans capture Vitebsk.
9–10 July	Germans cross the River Dniepr. Germans are now 10 miles from Kiev.
13–16 July	Germans reach the Luga River, 60 miles from Leningrad.
15 July	Smolensk falls.
30 July	Russians cut off at Uman.
5 August	Smolensk pocket reduced. Rumanians begin siege of Odessa.
8 August	Germans advance from the Luga bridgeheads.
16 August	Germans reach Novgorod and cross the River Volkhov.
30 August–2 September	Russian counter offensive fails.
1 September	German artillery opens up on Leningrad.
15 September	German panzers meet at Lokhvitsa, trapping four Russian armies around Kiev. Leningrad is encircled and the siege begins.
17 September	Stalin orders a withdrawal from Kiev.
18–27 September	Huge slaughter in the Kiev pocket. By now over 60 per cent of the Russian Army has been destroyed.
26 September	Hitler orders Operation *Typhoon*, the capture of Moscow.
2 October	Operation *Typhoon* launched.
7 October	Germans cut off Russian troops around Vyazma and Bryansk.
8 October	Rainy season begins.
14 October	Vyazma pocket destroyed.
20 October	Bryansk pocket eliminated.
20–25 October	Russian resistance begins to stiffen in front of Moscow.

23–24 October	Germans enter Kharkov.
9 November	The Tikhvin railhead falls to the Germans.
15 November	Moscow offensive halted due to cold weather and Russian resistance.
27 November	Germans are within 9 miles of Moscow and halted by fierce counterattacks.
28 November	Germans retire from Rostov after Russian counterattacks.
5 December	Hitler agrees to abandon the Moscow offensive and allows retreat to defensive positions.
5–6 December	Russian counteroffensive launched to relieve Moscow.
9 December	The Tikhvin railhead is recaptured.

Bibliography

Chamberlain, Peter and Chris Ellis, *Tanks of the World 1915 to 1945*, Arms and Armour Press, 1972.

Davis, Brian L, *German Army Uniforms and Insignia 1933 to 1945*, Arms and Armour Press, 1973.

Fowler, Will, *Russia 1941 to 1942*, Ian Allan, 2003.

Glantz, David M., *Barbarossa: Hitler's Invasion of Russia 1941*, Tempus, 2001.

Grove, Eric, *Russian Armour 1941 to 1943*, Almark, 1976.

Mollo, Andrew, *The Armed Forces of World War Two*, Orbis, 1981.

Sutherland, Jonathan, *World War Two Tanks and AFVs*, Airlife, 2002.

White, B.T., *Tanks and Other AFVs of the Blitzkrieg Era*, Blandford, 1972.

Notes

Notes

Notes

Notes

Notes

Notes

Notes

Notes

Notes

Notes